THE CALL OF DUTY
CAREERS IN THE
ARMED FORCES™

YOUR CAREER IN
THE ARMY

JASON PORTERFIELD

ROSEN
PUBLISHING®
New York

Published in 2012 by The Rosen Publishing Group, Inc.
29 East 21st Street, New York, NY 10010

Copyright © 2012 by The Rosen Publishing Group, Inc.

First Edition

Library of Congress Cataloging-in-Publication Data

Porterfield, Jason.
Your career in the army/Jason Porterfield.—1st ed.
  p. cm.—(The call of duty: careers in the armed forces)
Includes bibliographical references and index.
ISBN 978-1-4488-5510-0 (library binding)
1. United States. Army—Juvenile literature. 2. United States. Army—Vocational guidance—Juvenile literature. I. Title.
UA25.P67 2012
355.0023'73—dc22

                                                     201101324

Manufactured in the United States of America

CPSIA Compliance Information: Batch #W12YA: For further information, contact Rosen Publishing, New York, New York, at 1-800-237-9932.

CONTENTS

INTRODUCTION

On one side of the globe, an army scout vehicle leaves a base to carry out a dangerous reconnaissance mission. The soldiers in the vehicle are linked to the base that they just left through several communication channels. During their mission, they may drive on army-built roads and use information gathered by soldiers who specialize in gathering intelligence to safely navigate over terrain.

When they return, they are greeted by the military policemen guarding the entrance checkpoint. They proceed to make their report to their commanding officer. If they are wounded or injured, trained medical staff from the base infirmary see to their care, while skilled mechanics repair their vehicle.

On the other side of the world, army engineers may be planning improvements to a dam. Army counselors work with families of soldiers who have been deployed overseas. Drill sergeants mold the next generation of recruits. Even in peacetime, soldiers stay busy keeping the United States secure.

The army is a massive organization made up of many different parts. Soldiers in every field are expected to perform at the highest level at all times. The army places particular emphasis on its seven core

Army recruits begin their separation from the civilian world as soon as they enter basic training. During this period, drill sergeants mold them through hard work and discipline.

values: loyalty, duty, respect, selfless service, honor, integrity, and personal courage.

An army career can be the perfect path for men and women who work hard to excel at everything they do. The service can instill discipline and confidence. Soldiers may find that they thrive under the pressure of constant high expectations. During their service, soldiers are constantly given opportunities to improve their skills and get more training. By taking advantage of these opportunities, they get the chance to rise in the ranks and earn the respect of their peers and officers.

When soldiers leave the army, they will be prepared to face a wide range of challenges. Army programs can help them establish their civilian lives and find jobs that will utilize their training. The army also provides veterans with medical care and offers programs to help with the transition to civilian life.

CHAPTER 1

ENLISTING IN THE ARMY

Joining the U.S. Army is not a decision to take lightly. Enlistees are essentially giving four years of their lives to the service of their country. At the same time, the army can give them a place to learn new skills. By serving, they become part of a larger family of servicemen.

There are many benefits to serving. Soldiers are highly trained in their army jobs, also called military occupational specialties (MOS). The skills they learn often translate easily to civilian careers. Many companies specifically seek out military personnel because of their training and the discipline they learned while serving. Soldiers can also receive education benefits like the G.I. Bill that will help them pay for a college education or professional training when their service is up.

During their time in the army, soldiers have their basic needs looked after. They are fed and clothed by the army. Their housing is provided for, even if they have a family and live off base. The army also takes care of their medical needs.

However, army life is not for everyone. Soldiers have to get used to the idea that someone of a higher rank will always be able to give them orders and expect them to obey. They have to remember that their military career is not like a civilian job. Quitting is not an option if they are not happy with their work. Soldiers must always perform their jobs at a high level or risk punishment, even for showing up late to do their jobs.

Soldiers also have to adjust to being in places they may not want to be for long periods of time. They may wind up thousands of miles from their families for months on end. Life on a base can be extremely boring, and soldiers are not at liberty to leave the grounds anytime they want.

There is also the possibility of facing combat. Soldiers serving in a time of war can be killed or seriously injured in battle. They may see their friends get hurt or die. They may have to kill or wound other people. Even if those things do not happen, living in a war zone is extremely stressful. Soldiers get little time to rest and are constantly exposed to danger. They have to be constantly looking out for themselves and their comrades while staying focused on the job they have to perform. Soldiers exposed to such conditions may develop post-traumatic stress disorder (PTSD).

A recruiter talks to high school students about careers in the army. Recruiters who visit high schools can be a good source of information about the enlistment process.

QUALIFICATIONS

The army accepts many types of people into its ranks, but there are a few basic qualifications that must be met. Enlistees must be eighteen or older, although seventeen-year-olds can enlist if they have permission from their parents. On the other end, recruits must ship to basic training before they turn forty-two.

Soldiers must also be U.S. citizens or legal permanent immigrants living within the United States.

Those living outside the United States are not allowed to enlist. Recruits also need a criminal record that is free of serious felony offenses, such as murder, perjury, kidnapping, or burglary. All recruits must also be medically fit and pass medical standards handed down by the Department of Defense.

One of the most controversial Department of Defense standards was a prohibition against gay and lesbian soldiers serving openly. Called "Don't Ask, Don't Tell," the policy was put into place in 1993. Under the law, gay and lesbian soldiers could serve as long as they concealed their sexual orientation. Many who could not or would not hide their orientation were discharged. President Barack Obama signed a bill repealing the policy in December 2010.

Over the years, military statistics have shown that recruits who do not have a high school diploma are less likely to complete their training. All branches of the service are strict on requiring that recruits be high school graduates or at least hold a Graduate Equivalent Degree (GED). The army limits the number of GED holders it takes each year to no more than 10 percent, and those recruits must score much higher on the Armed Services Vocational Aptitude Battery (ASVAB) than high school graduates. Recruits with a GED who have at least fifteen college credits are placed in the same enlistment category as high school graduates.

MEETING WITH A RECRUITER

Once you've decided to join the army, the first step is to meet with a recruiter. Recruiting offices are located in cities and towns throughout the country. Recruiters sometimes come to high schools and job fairs to meet with students interested in joining the military. At those events, they may answer questions about their own service, provide brochures, and give out contact information.

Recruiters are held to high standards of accuracy. During the initial meeting, they will ask many detailed questions about a recruit's background, education, health, and family to form an idea of whether the recruit is suited for the army. Recruits also are weighed to see if they meet army standards, and they must take a sample ASVAB to show how they might do on the real exam.

Recruits should not be too nervous or afraid to ask questions when speaking with a recruiter. Recruiters are used to asking questions that may seem highly personal but are necessary to determine if a person belongs in the service. Likewise, recruiters are accustomed to answering questions about army life and helping recruits understand the commitment they are about to make.

It is a good idea to have a list of questions ready to ask. Remember to treat the recruiter with respect and use his or her proper title. Be polite and candid when answering questions. Making a good impression could help recruits who may need to ask for a waiver if they do not meet enlistment requirements. The information that the recruiter gathered will be sent to his or her superiors, and the recruit's medical history will go to a Military Entrance Processing Station (MEPS), where it will be reviewed by a doctor.

After the first meeting, recruits should take time to think about what they learned. They may find that they are not able to commit to serving, or that they are not ready and want to do something else with their lives first. They may not be willing to face the possibility of combat or be separated from their families during long deployments. The decision should not be rushed.

Joining the military can be like an extended job interview, and recruits may meet with their recruiters several times before the process is complete. At future meetings, recruits will have to bring along personal documents, including a birth certificate, driver's license, academic transcripts, diplomas, medical records, any court documents, and a list of references. These documents are necessary if the recruit is applying for a waiver. The army will do a background check to determine that the recruit is who he or she claims, and any necessary waiver processes will begin.

Army recruiters spend time getting to know recruits. They gather information by asking questions about the applicants' lives and histories, as well as answering questions from recruits.

The recruitment office can also be the point at which recruits choose their army career through a program called the Future Soldier Remote Reservation System. Any applicant with a high school diploma or who is a high school senior in good standing can select the army job of his or her choice from the system, though the applicant will have to meet the ASVAB and physical requirements for the job before it can be guaranteed.

When eligibility has been confirmed, the recruiter will make an appointment for the recruit to go to a MEPS. The station is where the recruit's real qualifications for joining the army will be assessed.

THE MEPS PROCESS

There are sixty-five MEPS located around the country and staffed by personnel from all five branches of the military. The process usually takes two days. Recruits are usually assigned to the MEPS nearest to them but may have to stay overnight in a hotel. The army usually has contracts with area hotels, so recruits will be able to stay for free or at a reduced rate.

Recruits who have not already taken the ASVAB will have to take the test the afternoon they arrive. The nine-section multiple-choice test is used by all branches of the military to assess the abilities of recruits. Subjects covered on the test are: word knowledge, arithmetic reasoning, mechanical comprehension, mechanical and shop information, electronic information, mathematics knowledge, general science, paragraph comprehension, and assembling objects. The test is offered in high schools to students in the tenth, eleventh, and twelfth grades, so many recruits will likely have already taken it.

The second day of the MEPS process starts with a wake-up call at about 5:30 AM. Recruits must report to the station by 6:00 AM and be prepared to stay as

10 QUESTIONS TO ASK A

ARMY RECRUITER

1. What benefits will I receive for enlisting?
2. Will I be able to communicate with family and friends during boot camp?
3. How long is my obligation to the army?
4. Will I be able to get the MOS that I want?
5. Will the army take care of my family if something happens to me?
6. What can I do to prepare for joining the army?
7. How will military service help me in the future?
8. How can I use the skills I learn in the army to get a civilian job?
9. What are the health and fitness requirements for joining?
10. What equipment, services, and benefits will I have to pay for while in the army?

late as 5:30 PM. They should arrive early after a good night's sleep and take along their Social Security card, driver's license, and birth certificate, as well as their eyeglasses or contact lenses, if needed. They will need to remove any piercings and should not wear clothes with obscene words or images.

The phrase "Hurry up and wait" is often used to describe the MEPS process. Recruits are often exposed to frustrating and stressful situations during the process and thus should expect to be dealt with strictly. Every step of the process is drawn out; recruits should be prepared to spend a great deal of time waiting. However, they are usually allowed to talk to one another and read, since magazines and books are not forbidden.

Recruits are searched and have to pass through a metal detector as they enter the station. Those who are allowed in are photographed and issued a bar-coded sticker. No gum, water, food, soda, or tobacco products are allowed, and recruits cannot wear hats, hoods, baggy or torn jeans, or shirts with large logos. Jewelry is also forbidden. Personnel at the station will take coats, any electronic devices, jewelry, and other valuables and lock them in a semisecure room until it is time to leave.

In between the long periods of waiting, recruits are put through a number of medical tests. Their heart rate and blood pressure are checked right away to

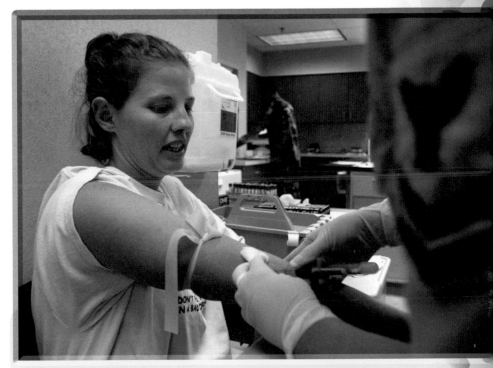

The MEPS process includes many physical and medical tests. New recruits must be able to meet army physical standards before going on to face the rigors of basic training.

exclude anyone with a rapid pulse or hypertension, and their breath is measured for alcohol. They fill out medical forms similar to those they saw in the recruiter's office and then undergo vision and hearing tests, a urine test for drugs, a thorough physical exam, weight check, and body-fat measurements.

The medical testing can take up most of the morning. Any scars, tattoos, or piercings are recorded. Recruits also undergo twenty-five physically awkward

ENLISTING AS A COMMISSIONED OFFICER

The vast majority of soldiers join the army as enlisted personnel. However, a few join as officers. There are two ways to enter as an officer from college: graduate from the U.S. Military Academy at West Point, New York, or take part in a Reserve Officers' Training Corps (ROTC) program in college.

Admission to West Point is extremely competitive. To get into the four-year college, students are usually nominated by a member of Congress. The academy seeks students who excel academically and are well rounded, as demonstrated by participating in sports and taking leadership roles in extracurricular activities. Graduates earn a degree in engineering or liberal arts and enter the army with the rank of second lieutenant.

ROTC programs can be found at three hundred institutions and through agreements with more than one thousand colleges and universities. ROTC students practice drills, dress in uniform, and are held to high standards of behavior. Students can leave the program at any time with no military obligation.

bone and muscle tests to demonstrate their range of movement. At the end of the medical exams, a physician declares recruits fit to serve if no obvious problems arise. Recruits are then fingerprinted, and the prints are used to check for any outstanding arrest warrants.

Doctors can medically disqualify a recruit if he or she fails to meet any one of the standards. The disqualification can be either temporary or permanent. Temporary disqualification means that the recruit may be able to join at a later date, such as if he or she is recovering from a recent injury. Recruits who are permanently disqualified are those who do not meet the published standards and their conditions are not expected to change. They can join the army only if they receive a medical waiver.

THE SECURITY INTERVIEW

Recruits who pass the medical exams are then subjected to a security clearance interview. The interview is part of a larger security clearance investigation conducted by the army, which looks into a recruit's character, reliability, loyalty, and trustworthiness. The investigation emphasizes the recruit's character and conduct in order to determine if he or she is eligible for access to national security information. Factors such as honesty, financial responsibility, emotional stability, and reliability are checked. The investigation includes credit and national records checks and can include interviews with people who know the recruit.

Most army careers require some level of security clearance, or soldiers wouldn't be able to do their work. Recruits have to be U.S. citizens in order to receive security clearance. Noncitizens can join the army, but their career options will be severely limited.

The interviewer asks many questions that may seem to have little to do with the army, but the answers help the interviewer decide whether a recruit is worthy of receiving security clearance. Many of the questions will seem similar to the questions asked by the recruiter. Interviewers will ask recruits about their finances, mental health, drug and alcohol use, and criminal history.

The answers will influence the level of clearance that a recruit is eligible for and the jobs available to him or her. Information is classified as confidential, secret, and top secret, with the most potentially damaging information being in the top-secret category. Recruits who are given top-secret clearance will have the widest range of army careers to choose from.

SIGNING THE ENLISTMENT AGREEMENT

Recruits meet with a service counselor/liaison to discuss the enlistment agreement. The counselor goes through the agreement line by line to make sure that recruits understand the various enlistment options and any enlistment benefits they qualify for under the job they selected. If a recruit failed to qualify for the job that he or she wanted, the counselor will go over other options.

Army recruits take their oath of enlistment during a special ceremony at a baseball game between the Tampa Bay Devil Rays and the San Diego Padres.

The army offers recruits active-duty service contracts for two years, three years, four years, five years, or six years. Few army jobs are available for the two-year or three-year enlistment tours, so most soldiers end up serving for four years or longer. All soldiers, even those with only a two-year contract, have a total service obligation of eight years. During this period, they are part of the army's Individual Ready Reserve (IRR) and thus can be called back into service until the eighth anniversary of their enlistment if needed.

After the meeting, recruits are fingerprinted and take the oath of enlistment. At this point, they are subject to army orders, standards, and regulations. Recruits are entered into a Direct Ship program, in which they report to basic training within two days to two months of completing the MEPS process and taking their oath, or they go into the Delayed Entry Program (DEP).

Under the DEP, recruits can wait anywhere from a week to several months before receiving orders to report to boot camp. The army recruits months in advance of its anticipated needs, so recruits can wait months before having to report. During this time, they may meet with their recruiter several times and can even work toward getting promoted by completing a DEP task list and learning certain military subjects.

CHAPTER 2

BASIC AND SKILL TRAINING

B asic training is the intense and difficult period of physical and mental training that all U.S. military recruits must go through before joining the armed forces. All five branches of the military have a basic training program geared to each branch's specialty. When recruits successfully finish, they emerge as highly trained and skilled soldiers dedicated to defending their country. From there, they go on to learn the specialty skills that the army needs in order to remain a highly advanced fighting force.

BASIC TRAINING

In the army, basic training lasts for nine weeks. When the army has an opening for a recruit's MOS, he or she is ordered to report to the MEPS and then to basic training at one of several bases. Even though recruits are not yet officially members of the army, the service agreement they signed requires that they report when ordered.

Soldiers undergoing basic training navigate an obstacle course at Fort Benning, Georgia. Obstacle course training is used to teach soldiers to work together toward a common goal.

Army basic training consists of two components: Basic Combat Training (BCT) and Advanced Individual Training (AIT). Where troops go for basic training depends on where training for their MOS takes place. Some recruits may go to one base for the combat training component and then have to travel to a second base for their advanced training, although the army tries to keep them geographically close. Others receive their basic training and specialty training at once in a program called One Station Unit Training (OSUT).

BCT is what most people imagine when they think of basic training. During this phase, recruits are put through seemingly endless drills and exercises designed to bring them to their peak physical conditioning and teach them to work with other soldiers. This instruction is led by a drill sergeant, who shows them the ropes of army life and corrects them when necessary. Under the drill sergeant's watchful eye, recruits learn the basics of being a soldier, including military protocol and regulations and combat techniques.

Drill sergeants are trained to constantly assess a recruit's appearance, uniform, demeanor, attitude, and enthusiasm. If they see something they don't like, they will make the recruit correct the lapse. Often, the correction is accompanied by some form of punishment, such as additional exercises or more duties to perform. Recruits are expected to take any such punishment stoically.

Army basic training is physically demanding, so recruits should try to arrive in good physical condition. They should also become familiar with army ranks and regulations. Such knowledge will be useful and may help recruits avoid punishment. Also, recruits will only be allowed certain possessions while at basic training. Lists of permitted items will be available from the MEPS.

When recruits first arrive at basic training, they enter a phase called reception battalion, which lasts for four to ten days. Their initial preparations for basic training are made there. They get their haircut, receive uniforms and any gear they may need, and submit to another round of physical exams and a physical fitness test. Recruits are vaccinated and taught the basics of army life, such as how to march, how to stand, and barracks upkeep.

BCT is divided into three phases, with recruits qualifying for more responsibilities, privileges, and independence with the completion of each phase. During the first phase, recruits have virtually no independence or free time. They have to adjust to a rigid daily schedule and get used to performing many tasks under pressure and to high expectations.

Time is strictly regulated in basic training. Days typically run from a wake-up call at 5:00 AM to lights out at 9:30 PM. Soldiers have just a few minutes every morning to make their beds, get dressed, and make themselves presentable. Men are required to shave every morning.

Physical training starts at 5:30 AM, followed by breakfast at 6:30 AM, and more physical training from 8:30 AM to noon, when lunch is served. Training resumes from 1:00 to 5:00 PM, followed by dinner until 6:00 PM. From the end of dinner to 8:30 PM is "Drill Sergeant Time," during which the drill sergeant lectures

Soldiers at Fort Hamilton in New York City do push-ups as the sun rises. In basic training, every morning begins with vigorous physical exercise.

on any army-related subjects that he or she sees fit. After that, recruits get one hour of personal time in which they can do laundry, write letters, or relax.

Phase I, called "Red Phase," lasts for the first three weeks. During this time, drill sergeants have total control over the actions of recruits. This phase marks the beginning of intense physical training. Recruits also learn military customs and practices, the army's core values, drills, and ceremonies. During the second week, recruits will get their rifles and learn how to handle them, including taking them apart and cleaning them.

At the end of the third week, recruits are assigned to work closely with another recruit as a "battle buddy." The two recruits will spend nearly all of their time together and will share in any punishment. Recruits, even those who trained beforehand, will make mistakes during this phase. But by the end of this, they will have learned how to get things done the army way.

Phase II, or "White Phase," lasts from the fourth through sixth weeks and marks the point when recruits begin intensive weapons training. They will learn to fire their M16A2 rifles. At first, they will fire at stationary targets, eventually moving on to targets that are farther away or that pop up. They will also practice throwing grenades and using grenade launchers. During the second week, recruits are introduced to heavier weapons, such as antitank guns, and practice using their bayonets to stab and slash enemies.

Physical training will continue, and recruits will begin navigating obstacle courses. They carry their rifles with them on the course, and battle buddies are expected to help each other.

Phase III is the "Blue Phase" and marks the last three weeks of basic training. Recruits take a final physical training test that they must pass before they

Recruits practice taking their rifles apart and putting them back together as part of a basic training exercise. They must be able to put the weapons together quickly and correctly.

can move on with their platoon. By this time, recruits have gone through so much physical training that failing the test is rare.

For the second week, the recruits go out on a field exercise that includes sleeping in tents, eating MREs (meals ready-to-eat) out of trays, and experiencing simulated combat situations. When the exercise is over, they return to the base for a short, informal ceremony marking their final transition from civilians to soldiers. The final week is often called "recovery week." Recruits repair and service any equipment issued to them that they will not be taking to AIT, make sure the platoon barracks are in good shape to receive the next set of recruits, and practice for the formal graduation ceremony held at the end of the week.

ADJUNCT GENERAL CORPS, AIR DEFENSE ARTILLERY, AND U.S. ARMY ARMOR SCHOOLS

By the end of basic training, soldiers know how to handle army life. They will have spent weeks doing little but exercising, practicing army drills, and learning to work together as a unit. They move on from there to AIT to learn their MOS. At this point, they are considered to be in Phase IV of army training. As their training progresses, they are allowed more privileges and are eventually awarded Phase V privileges.

The AIT process for each new soldier depends on his or her MOS. Some MOS don't require much specialized training and are over in as few as three weeks. Others can take up to eighty-four weeks. There are seventeen AIT schools located at several army bases.

The Adjunct General Corps School located at Fort Jackson, South Carolina, is where soldiers learn how to support the army through personnel management.

Two soldiers zero in on a virtual enemy aircraft during a training exercise. Modern weapons training for soldiers includes the use of virtual reality technology to simulate combat conditions.

The training available at this school includes combat readiness, strength reporting, casualty operations, replacement management, information management, postal operations, morale, welfare and recreation support, and personnel services. They are also trained in offering support to the families of soldiers.

Career fields that are covered by this training include human resources, financial services, and administration. Soldiers in these fields often work behind the scenes, but their jobs have a huge impact on the army's ability to carry out its mission. They help soldiers with tasks affecting their overall welfare and well-being while keeping them combat-ready. Specific schools here are the Army School of Music, Finance School, the Noncommissioned Officers Academy, and the Recruiting and Retention School.

The Air Defense Artillery School is one of the army's most technologically advanced training programs. Based at Fort Sill, Oklahoma, the school specializes in evolving to meet the threat of air and missile attacks. Soldiers train in the Patriot missile system and the Avenger system.

The army's Armor School is at Fort Knox, Kentucky. Soldiers at this school learn how to carry out combat operations involving tanks and other tracked vehicles. They train in tactics, operations, repair, and maintenance of heavy vehicles like the M1 Abrams tank and the Bradley Fighting Vehicle. They also learn to use personal weapons and support equipment such as radios, as well as how to conduct surveillance.

AVIATION LOGISTICS AND CHEMICAL SCHOOLS

Soldiers at the Aviation Logistics School at Fort Eustis, Virginia, learn how to repair and maintain the army's helicopters. Their training and knowledge are vital to keeping army forces in the sky. They gain a working knowledge of the aircraft and their systems and parts. Eventually, they become specialized in the AH-64 Apache, the UH-60 Blackhawk, the CH-47 Chinook, or the OH-50 Kiowa.

The army's Chemical School is located at Fort Leonard Wood, Missouri. Here, soldiers learn how to detect and identify chemical, biological, radiological, and nuclear weapons, as well as how to operate vehicles and equipment related to chemical, biological, radiological, and nuclear operations. They train in reconnaissance, decontamination, and smoke operations.

DEPARTMENT OF DEFENSE FIRE ACADEMY

This academy is for all branches of the military, and soldiers here learn many of the same skills as civilian firefighters. They train in fire protection fundamentals, fire alarm communications, building construction, fire behavior and prevention, emergency medical care, responder care, and structural firefighting principles. They also learn about forcible entry, ropes, knots, rescue practices, rescue activities and vehicle extrication, ladder and ventilation practices, hazardous material response, and aircraft rescue firefighting.

Soldiers who complete this AIT receive Firefighter II certification and are trained to handle hazardous material accidents and other fire operations, as well as work as aircraft rescue firefighters. Their courses are college accredited and accredited by the Department of Defense.

ENGINEER, FIELD ARTILLERY, FINANCE CORPS, AND INFANTRY SCHOOLS

The army's Engineer School is located at Fort Leonard Wood as well. Soldiers learn a wide variety of engineering skills, including bridge building, structural maintenance, and electrical engineering.

Soldiers specializing in field artillery attend Field Artillery School at Fort Sill, where they train to use a variety of weapons systems and munitions. They train in tactics, techniques, and procedures for using artillery in support of other soldiers.

Soldiers who attend Finance Corps School at Fort Jackson learn how to support soldiers and commanders by providing timely and accurate accounting and financial services. These services include making sure that soldiers get paid, preparing and paying travel expenses and vendor vouchers, and accounting for public funds. They also learn to

Army engineers work together to guide sections of a bridge into position during a training exercise. Combat forces rely on engineers to provide infrastructure in hostile environments.

support logistical, medical, and supply requirements during missions.

Soldiers at Infantry School become members of combat teams that use small arms, antiarmor, and indirect fire weapons. Their training is combined with basic training in OSUT at Fort Benning, Georgia. They learn to operate and maintain weapons, how to read maps, navigate, and perform reconnaissance

A sergeant from the army's Unmanned Aircraft Systems Training Battalion demonstrates how to use a UAS simulator to replicate possible combat conditions.

missions, minefield safety, and how to prepare fighting positions, build barriers, and operate communications equipment.

MILITARY INTELLIGENCE AND MILITARY POLICE SCHOOL

Military intelligence soldiers are responsible for gathering intelligence during missions. At Military Intelligence School at Fort Huachuca, Arizona, they learn to collect intelligence through interviews and from digital sources, such as photos taken by unmanned aerial vehicles (UAVs). They also learn to prepare and present intelligence for their superiors and how to recognize its place in larger missions.

Military police maintain law, order, and discipline as a means of providing security for army personnel. They undergo training at Military Police School

DRILL SERGEANT

Soldiers usually remember their drill sergeants as extremely tough and impossible to please. The army chooses only its best sergeants to attend Drill Sergeant School in Fort Jackson. Drill sergeants must go through a rigorous training program that mimics every step of basic training so that the experience is fresh in their minds.

Drill sergeants have to mold raw recruits into capable soldiers. To do their job, they have to become the best of the best in all aspects of military life, from making beds and marching to firing weapons. They learn how to use their authority to get the best results from recruits and how to become role models for generations of soldiers.

at Fort Leonard Wood, where they train to provide security, antiterrorism, and force protection and to handle and investigate crimes committed on army installations.

ORDNANCE MECHANICAL MAINTENANCE SCHOOL

Soldiers who attend the army's Ordnance Mechanical Maintenance School at Fort Lee, Virginia, learn to ensure that weapons systems, vehicles, and tactical

U.S. soldiers destroy a surface-to-air missile captured from Iraqi forces in 2003. Such risky jobs require precision from explosive ordnance personnel, army engineers, and specialists.

support equipment are ready to use and in good working order. They learn how to perform mechanical and electrical maintenance on tanks, weapons, Humvees, trucks, mobile power generators, and air conditioners. They also learn to repair and maintain noncombat equipment such as laundry and water purification systems, pumps, heaters, and decontamination equipment. While in the army, these soldiers can earn certification with accrediting agencies, and many of the skills they learn can be applied to college credits.

Ordnance Munitions and Electronic Maintenance School

Soldiers at this school, located at Redstone Arsenal, Alabama, learn how to dispose of explosives, maintain electronics and missiles, and how to manage ammunition. The school offers civilian-accredited, college-level curricula and allows soldiers to gain experience in disarming explosive devices with remote-control robots, repairing electronic systems of radar and missile systems, and transporting explosive munitions.

Quartermaster, Signal Corps, and Transportation Schools

Soldiers attending Quartermaster School at Fort Lee learn about providing troops with necessities such as food, water, and repair parts. Their training includes strategies for supporting troops at war and during peacetime. They also learn to work with other branches of the military and with forces from other countries.

The Signal Corps supplies information systems and worldwide networks for the U.S. Army, the Department of Defense, and allied nations. Soldiers in the Signal Corps train at Fort Gordon, Georgia, where they develop the skills to automate, transmit, and receive information useful to the army. They study in one of three areas: information systems operations, signal (communications) operations, and visual operations.

Soldiers at Transportation School, located at Fort Lee, learn to operate and maintain army tactical trucks, watercraft, and material handling equipment. They learn about traffic management, convoy operations, cargo transfers, documenting cargo, sailing and maintenance of army vessels, and unloading aircraft, ships, railcars, and trucks.

CHAPTER 3

HEALTH CARE AND HUMAN SERVICES CAREERS

S oldiers sign up to serve in the army with the full expectation that all of their health care needs are going to be covered. To meet this expectation, the army provides top-flight training and state-of-the-art equipment for its medical personnel. Depending on their skills, specialty, and level of education, soldiers can find themselves in positions ranging from performing emergency surgery in a field hospital near a combat zone to practicing a specialty on a base in the United States.

Enlisted health care practitioners within the Medical Command (MEDCOM) are trained to provide medical care to military personnel on and off the field. They assist nurses, surgeons, and physicians with medical procedures and provide emergency care during combat, as well as assistance during routine medical exams. Soldiers who choose this career field should have a high level of compassion and a willingness to help others.

In a special exercise at Fort Sam Houston, Texas, combat medics are trained to administer aid to the wounded while also watching out for hidden dangers.

The army's medical training takes place at MEDCOM's headquarters, located at Fort Sam Houston, Texas. Training varies according to specific job requirements. Because of the broad scope of the army's medical needs for soldiers, their families, and civilian personnel, a wide range of medical careers are available. Some involve working directly with patients, while others require working with equipment or handling administrative duties.

BIOMEDICAL EQUIPMENT

Specialists in biomedical equipment are responsible for servicing and maintaining all medical equipment. The devices they work with may have mechanical, hydraulic, digital, pneumatic, optical, electronic, and even radiological components. Duties for these specialists include installing and servicing equipment, figuring out space and power requirements, performing maintenance checks, making repairs, and preparing equipment reports. As they gain more experience and rise in the ranks, they may help develop these procedures, perform inspections, and advise and supervise other technicians.

Soldiers in this field must have forty-one weeks of AIT in the classroom and the field. This training includes practice in repairing and replacing parts. During AIT, technicians learn the principles of electronics and how to use and maintain electrical and electronic test equipment.

In civilian life, these skills could translate into electronics repair work in the fields of manufacturing, medical research, satellite communications, or commercial airline companies. With some additional training, these soldiers can qualify for professional certification at several levels.

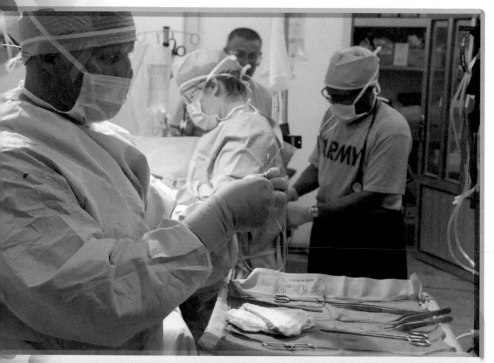

Operating room specialists are vital to carrying out successful medical procedures. They must be familiar with the equipment and instruments in use and are responsible for keeping everything sterile.

OPERATING ROOM SPECIALIST

Operating room specialists step in to provide emergency help to injured or wounded soldiers when doctors aren't available. They help nurses prepare patients and the operating room for surgery, assist during surgery, and are responsible for keeping medical supplies and special equipment sterile. They also help manage operating room suites. In an advanced role, they may set up and operate medical equipment and supervise other specialists.

After basic training, these specialists receive nineteen weeks of AIT and on-the-job instruction. They study the human body and learn emergency medical treatment procedures and basic nursing care, minor surgical procedures, clinical laboratory procedures, and how to diagnose diseases.

Postmilitary careers include work with civilian hospitals, clinics, nursing homes, and rehabilitation centers. A background as an operating room specialist can lay the groundwork for a career as a medical assistant, medication aide, or physician's assistant. After finishing AIT, these specialists also have the chance to pursue professional certification as a certified surgical technologist.

DENTAL AND OPTICAL LAB SPECIALISTS

Dental care is one of the services available to army personnel all over the world. Dental specialists help army dentists examine and treat soldiers and maintain their offices.

Their duties include helping care for patients, receiving patients, preparing exam rooms, and selecting and arranging instruments. They also measure and record patient temperature, blood pressure, and pulse,

A dental specialist conducts a dental examination on an Afghan man at a clinic near Shindand, Afghanistan. Army medical personnel overseas often provide treatment services for local residents.

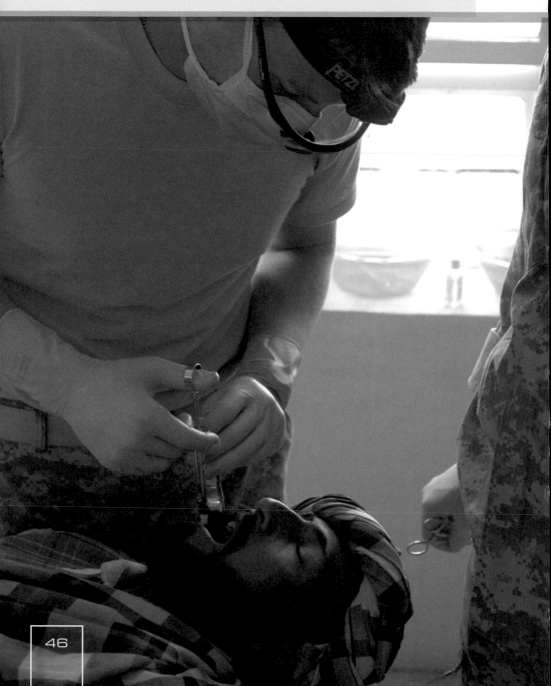

and help administer anesthesia and place and remove sutures. Administrative tasks, such as scheduling appointments, filing, and maintaining records, are also their responsibility.

Dental specialists must go through thirty weeks of AIT in the classroom and in the field. They learn preventive dentistry, X-ray techniques, office procedures, and dental hygiene procedures. This training and their army experience can prepare them for a career as a dental assistant or dental hygienist. With some additional study, they can gain certification with the American Medical Technologists as a registered dental assistant or with the Dental Assisting National Board as a certified dental assistant.

Optical laboratory specialists make and repair the eyeglasses issued to army personnel. They grind and shape lenses, assemble spectacles, and maintain the necessary tools and equipment. This specialty requires twenty-four weeks of AIT, during which they learn optics, ocular anatomy, and the technical skills needed to make glasses.

These soldiers should have an interest in biology and the industrial arts, as well as an interest in work requiring close attention to detail and the ability to use precision tools and instruments. This work prepares soldiers for work in optical labs and as optician's assistants. With some additional training, they may be able to pursue a career as an optician.

NUTRITION CARE

Nutrition care specialists help supervise medical nutrition care operations. They treat patients in nutrition clinics, clinical dietetics branches, and health promotion and wellness clinics. They also perform nutritional assessments and screen individual patients for nutritional risk, as well as prepare and serve modified and regular food fitting the nutrition needs of soldiers.

These soldiers go through a seven-week AIT course, during which they practice preparing food, learn standard and dietetic recipes, learn how to order food and supplies, and how to store perishable food. Soldiers in this specialty will have the knowledge and experience necessary to work at a variety of dining facilities.

OTHER POSITIONS FOR ENLISTED SOLDIERS

Other positions include medical logistics specialists, who are in charge of medical supplies and inventories; veterinary food inspection specialists; respiratory specialists; and pharmacy specialists.

Animals play important roles even in today's modern army, and animal care specialists are responsible for the welfare of dogs, horses, and sea mammals.

COMBAT MEDICS

Combat medics are among a class of soldiers called health care specialists. They go into combat zones to provide immediate treatment to wounded personnel. Combat medics must work quickly to stabilize injured and wounded soldiers long enough to get them to a field hospital or other available facility. They must perform calmly in extremely stressful situations and often put themselves in dangerous situations in order to save the lives of their fellow soldiers.

Combat medics train for sixteen weeks in emergency medicine techniques and learn aspects of inpatient care. Once they are sent to a unit, they may be assigned to study advanced topics or specialties. Frontline combat medics may study advanced treatments for trauma, while those who are assigned to medical units may learn how to administer medication.

Radiology specialists are trained to take X-rays of patients, a skill that requires twenty-four weeks of AIT. Preventive medicine specialists are responsible for preventing the spread of disease and infection through inspections, surveys, and implementation of preventive medicine lab procedures.

The Army Medical Department (AMEDD) is one of the world's largest and most advanced health care systems. Doctors and medical specialists who join the AMEDD enter as officers and do not go through the same basic training process as other recruits. They attend an Officer Basic Course (OBC) at Fort Sam Houston consisting of a basic orientation in the health care system and the army way of life.

Training time for these officers lasts ten to fourteen weeks and depends on the chosen specialty and whether they have previous military experience. They must also meet height requirements and pass the army's physical fitness test, as well as meet any requirements needed to enter their corps.

As highly trained as the army's health care workers may be, there are spiritual and psychological wounds that they cannot heal. This is where the human services soldiers are needed. Human services enlisted personnel provide counseling and spiritual support for soldiers, working with psychologists, social workers, and chaplains to organize treatment, classes, and religious services. Soldiers in this field need excellent communication and organizational skills, but no previous religious or medical training is required.

The chaplain assistant field is open to soldiers of high moral character who want to provide religious support for soldiers and their families. They help chaplains coordinate religious services for all faiths and carry out their duties in the field and on base,

including taking care of battlefield casualties. They
also see to administrative tasks, counsel their peers,
and act as the chaplain's driver and armed guard.

Chaplain assistants undergo seven weeks of AIT.
They study religious history and background information and learn about the chaplain's duties. They
also learn typing and writing skills and how to fill out
army forms.

COUNSELING JOBS FOR OFFICERS

The army trains some officers to provide emotional
and spiritual support to soldiers through counseling, social work, and religious services. Many officers
in this field have prior training as social workers,
psychologists, or practitioners of a specific religious
tradition.

Chaplains are the army's spiritual leaders. Unlike
chaplain assistants, they must be confirmed and
endorsed members of their faith. Because they will
likely be taking care of soldiers from a variety of religious backgrounds, they need to be sensitive to their
religious needs as well. Chaplains must have a college
degree with at least 120 hours of study and a graduate
degree in theological or religious studies. They need a
minimum of two years of professional experience and
must be at least twenty-one, yet younger than forty-five.

Clinical psychologists provide mental health
care to soldiers and their families. Before joining

An army chaplain says the benediction following a prayer service for American soldiers at a base in Zabul Province, Afghanistan.

the army, they need to have a doctoral degree in clinical psychology, counseling psychology, or some other subspecialty. They must be between the ages of twenty-one and forty-two and need a current and unrestricted license to practice.

Social workers are responsible for ensuring the well-being of troops and their families. Their duties can include supervision, research, teaching, training, and policy development. They must have a master's degree in social work from a program accredited with the Council on Social Work Education. The age and licensing requirements are the same as for clinical psychologists.

CHAPTER 4

INFORMATION TECHNOLOGY

Latitude
Longitude

The U.S. Army is dedicated to staying on the cutting edge of technology and thus has invested heavily in information and computer systems. Many modern weapons utilize complex computer and electronic components. The army will need more soldiers with skills in these areas as computers become more prominent in its operations. Soldiers in this field receive their AIT at Signal Corps School, located at Fort Gordon.

Military computers store and process a vast amount of data on subjects such as personnel, communications, finances, and the weather. They are used to operate equipment during peacetime and times of war. This equipment includes complex weapons and communications systems.

Soldiers trained in information and computer technology are responsible for making sure that the military's computer systems work properly. They are also responsible for ensuring that sensitive data remains safe behind firewalls and encryption programs. These positions will become even more important as computers become more vital to the army's mission.

An interest in mathematics and applying mathematical principles to solving problems is helpful in this field. Soldiers should also be able to communicate clearly and effectively and have an interest in work that requires accuracy and attention to detail.

INFORMATION TECHNOLOGY SPECIALIST

Information technology specialists maintain, process, and troubleshoot the army's computer systems and operations. They need a wide range of computer skills in order to get the job done. As network administrators, they install, configure, and monitor networks, hardware, and software, and they compile, enter, and process information. As programmers, they create and test computer programs.

There is a customer service aspect to their work. They identify problems that users have with computers and try to resolve them. They also help users with services such as passwords, e-mail accounts, troubleshooting, and security.

An instructor at the U.S. Army Signal Center Satellite Principles Transformation Trainer Lab shows a private how to perform a function on a satellite uplink.

To learn these skills, they undergo twenty weeks of AIT and hands-on training. The AIT course covers computer systems concepts, the use of computer consoles and peripheral equipment, and how to plan, design, and test computer systems. These skills translate easily into civilian work as a network support technician, data processing technician, or computer programmer.

SIGNAL SUPPORT SYSTEMS SPECIALIST

Signal support systems specialists maintain communication devices that help track troop movements. They work mainly with signal support systems and terminal devices to make sure that the right information is communicated correctly. They maintain electronic devices and install, operate, and maintain radio and data distribution systems. They offer training and assistance

A signal support systems specialist installs a transmitting unit for a Cheetah communications system in Afghanistan. The equipment allows personnel at remote locations to use the Internet or call the United States.

for users of automated telecommunication computer systems, for local area networks and routers, and for signal communications. Installing and maintaining signal support equipment and terminal devices are among their duties, as are operating and performing maintenance checks and services on vehicles and power generators.

Training for these specialists includes eighteen weeks of AIT and hands-on instruction, including practice with equipment. During their training, they learn mechanical, electronic, and electrical principles, maintenance procedures, techniques for installing and wiring electrical lines, and communications security policies and procedures. The training and experience will qualify soldiers for jobs with civilian companies that make and install radio equipment. Those who undertake additional study and accumulate two years of experience can qualify for professional certification as an associate certified electronics technician.

SATELLITE COMMUNICATIONS SYSTEMS OPERATOR-MAINTAINER

The army needs to have its communication lines up and running at all times. Satellite communications systems allow soldiers to stay in contact with each other in areas where other lines of communication may be difficult to set up.

Satellite communications systems operator-maintainers install, operate, maintain, and repair the army's multichannel satellite communications

Satellite team members work to hook up a quick reaction satellite antenna under the supervision of a satellite communications system operator-maintainer.

networks, including the Digital Communications Satellite Subsystem. They must be prepared to handle these vital communication lines at all times and in all conditions. They also have to be able to maintain their equipment and vehicles and install and operate necessary power generators.

Job training for this work includes up to twenty-six weeks of AIT, including time spent both in the classroom and under simulated battlefield conditions. These soldiers learn about satellite communications and how to work with codes and maintain communications equipment. The training is useful for soldiers who go on to work with communications equipment at hospitals, airports, police departments, and other organizations with large communications networks.

SIGNAL OFFICERS AND COMMUNICATIONS TECHNOLOGIST AND TECHNICIAN

The Signal Corps is responsible for all communications systems for the entire U.S. Army. Maintaining secure and consistent information systems and lines of communication at all levels of command is vital to the army's success.

Signal Corps officers are responsible for managing these systems. They have to be experts in planning, installing, operating, integrating, and maintaining voice, data, and information systems and services. They need a complete understanding of these technologies and should be highly intelligent.

A Signal Corps officer's responsibilities include planning and executing communication lines on missions during peacetime and while at war. They have to understand tactical decision-making and how to act as leaders in joint-force operations. They coordinate the use of signal soldiers at all levels of command.

Signal officers must complete a Signal Officer Basic Course (SOBC). They learn tactics, leadership skills, and maintenance and operational aspects of the communications systems and equipment they must use.

The army's many communications systems require constant attention from personnel trained to operate and maintain them. This equipment includes radios, telephones, antennas, satellites, and security and network devices. Enlisted personnel operate a variety of communications equipment, including radios, telephones, antennas, satellites, and security and network devices. These recruits should have technical and communications skills.

RADIO OPERATIONS

Soldiers can also operate radio communication devices, perform maintenance checks, and service their equipment. Their duties include maintaining, testing, and repairing communication gear and security devices; preparing and sending messages; and receiving and recording messages. They also install, operate, and maintain power generators.

Thirteen weeks of AIT are required for radio operator-maintainers, including time in the field and classroom sessions. They learn principles of mechanics and electricity, maintenance procedures, techniques for wiring and installing equipment, and policies for communications security. The training and experience they receive can help them in careers that involve installing and operating communications equipment or with firms that design and make such equipment.

Radio/communications security repairers are responsible for maintaining radio receivers, transmitters, communication security equipment, controlled cryptographic equipment, and other devices. Their duties include troubleshooting and repairing radio and communication security equipment, installing and repairing circuits and wiring, and calibrating and aligning equipment. They also test repaired equipment to make sure that it works properly.

Work in this field requires twenty-four weeks and two days of AIT and on-the-job instruction, with soldiers learning about wiring, mechanical and electrical principles, maintenance techniques, and communications security. The training and experience can prepare soldiers to qualify for certification with the Electronics Technician Association. When they leave

CYBER WARFARE

The army evolves constantly to respond to threats to the United States. One of the most prominent threats to emerge in recent years is the possibility of a cyber attack, in which data is stolen or systems are compromised to the point where they don't function properly. Such attacks by terrorists or enemy nations could result in the loss of valuable information and could harm the nation's infrastructure.

To combat the threat, the army has established its own Cyber Command as part of the U.S. Cyber Command. It pools the army's resources to ensure that policies, personnel, and resources can be made to work together in cyberspace. More than twenty-one thousand soldiers and civilians will eventually work under the Cyber Command.

the army, they may find work with civilian companies that design and make communications and electronic equipment or find jobs repairing such devices.

SPECIAL ELECTRONIC DEVICES REPAIRER

Special electronic devices repairers take care of the army's specialized electronics. They maintain and repair microcomputers and electromechanical telecommunications equipment, field artillery digital devices,

Special electronic devices repairers are responsible for maintaining specialized electronic equipment, such as the night-vision gear that this soldier is using to watch for illegal border crossings in Kosovo.

global positioning system (GPS) receivers, switch-boards, telephones and phone equipment, night-vision equipment, laser and fiber optic systems, and mine detection and dispensing systems. Other devices they may work on include gear used for measuring distance; battlefield illumination; and nuclear, biological, and chemical warning and measuring devices. They test, troubleshoot, and repair equipment, and perform quality-control measures and equipment inspections.

These soldiers go through twenty-five weeks of AIT, during which they practice repairing and replacing equipment parts in the classroom and in the field. Their training and some additional study can help them qualify for certification as an associate certified electronics technician with the Electronics Technician Association and can prepare them for a wide variety of technician positions after leaving the army.

MULTICHANNEL TRANSMISSION SYSTEMS OPERATOR-MAINTAINER

The army's strong communication network includes devices that communicate through more than one channel. Multichannel transmission systems operator-maintainers work directly on those devices and are responsible for installing, repairing, operating, and maintaining them, their antennae, and other related equipment. They run diagnostic tests on faulty equipment, install and maintain security devices, and take care of the vehicles and power generators that they need to do their jobs.

This work requires eighteen weeks of AIT, during which soldiers learn how to install and operate multichannel equipment and get hands-on experience with multichannel transmitters. They also learn how to operate equipment designed to diagnose problems with network switches and how to maintain transmission vehicles. As their careers continue, they take more classes and receive more advanced training. Their experience and training can lead to civilian careers with telecommunications companies, companies that sell specific communication networks, and government agencies that need their skills.

CAREERS FOR OFFICERS

Officers in the information technology field plan and direct communications operations, making sure that information gets to its source in a timely fashion. They are responsible for planning and directing communication operations, and they manage the personnel in communication centers and relay stations.

CHAPTER 5

CONSTRUCTION AND MECHANICS CAREERS

The army operates from a huge number of bases throughout the United States and around the world. Army construction crews are constantly working on new buildings and facilities, as well as maintaining and renovating existing ones. Enlisted construction personnel include bridge builders, plumbers, interior electricians, surveyors, water treatment specialists, and others. Army engineers plan and direct major projects vital to carrying out long-term and short-term missions, while machine support soldiers maintain vehicles and technologically advanced equipment.

In this field, enlisted personnel prepare land, dig foundations, and construct buildings for airfields, roads, dams, and other facilities. In some specialties, they may use heavy equipment, while others use power tools. Many of these jobs require a high level of technical training. Their work has to be durable

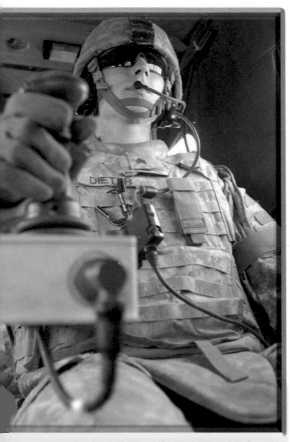

A combat engineer from the 688th Engineer Company monitors his Common Remotely Operated Weapon Station from the shelter of a mine-resistant, ambush-protected vehicle.

enough to endure hard use by personnel and sometimes must be carried out under stressful conditions, including combat.

COMBAT ENGINEER

Combat engineers work as part of a team to help army units stay as mobile as possible. They build fighting position fortifications, construct fixed and floating bridges, put up obstacles and defensive positions, and place and detonate explosives. They also help breach obstacles put up by enemy forces, carry out assaults against river crossings, demolish targets, and detect mines.

Their training requires fourteen weeks of OSUT, during which future combat engineers learn about basic demolitions and explosive hazards, urban operations, how to construct wire obstacles and build fixed bridges, and how to operate heavy equipment. The work prepares them for jobs in engineering, construction, and building inspection.

INTERIOR ELECTRICIAN

Interior electricians install and maintain electrical systems of up to six hundred volts. They have to read and interpret drawings, plans, and specifications. Their work includes many of the same tasks that a civilian electrician would perform, such as installing service panels, switches, electrical boxes, cables, conduit, and any necessary special equipment. They test circuits and inspect electrical systems and components and faulty equipment, making repairs in accordance with the National Electrical Code and any local laws.

These electricians receive seven weeks of AIT. During this time, they learn the fundamentals of electricity, safety procedures, wiring techniques, and how to troubleshoot malfunctioning circuits. The experience will prepare soldiers for civilian careers as independent electrical contractors or staff electricians.

BRIDGE CREWMEMBER

Soldiers often have to cope with treacherous terrain during combat operations. Bridge crews make it possible for soldiers to cross rivers, canyons, and other

Army water treatment specialists from the 1st Cavalry Division navigate a forklift through a designated area as part of a "Truck Rodeo" competition at Fort Hood, Texas.

landforms. Bridge crewmembers combine combat ability and building skill to overcome difficult terrain for crossing both wet and dry gaps. This work requires them to have good balance and agility, as well as the strength and endurance to do strenuous work over long periods of time.

They operate bridge trucks, which are vehicles that carry folding armored bridges that are designed to extend over gaps. They also launch and work as deck hands on bridgebuilding boats, requiring that they help handle shorelines, prepare the bridge site, and assist in rafting operations. Some of this work requires using heavy equipment. They also install devices that will demolish the bridges after they have been used, if necessary, and install barbed wire to serve as an obstacle to opposing forces.

Bridge crewmembers undergo fourteen weeks of one-station training, which includes nine weeks of basic training and five weeks of specialized training. They learn basic construction skills and engineering principles, bridgebuilding and road repair skills, rough carpentry and rigging, and how to operate power tools. This experience can qualify soldiers for civilian jobs in construction fields.

WATER TREATMENT

Army water treatment specialists inspect facilities and food supplies for germs, diseases, and other health and environmental hazards. They are responsible for installing and operating water purification equipment. They also oversee water storage and distribution. In the field, they help with reconnaissance missions to find water sources and prepare sites for encampments. They help set up the water treatment equipment, which they operate and maintain. They also store drinkable water, issue it to soldiers, and perform quality analysis tests.

U.S. ARMY CORPS OF ENGINEERS

The mission of the U.S. Army Corps of Engineers is to provide public engineering services to help protect the nation's security, boost the economy, and reduce risks from disasters. The corps builds structures, devises civil works programs, works to manage national resources, and provides combat support. In the United States, the corps' most visible work is dams, canals, and flood control systems. It is heavily involved in efforts to improve waterways and shorelines.

More than thirty-four thousand soldiers and civilians work for the corps. To become an army engineer, a soldier must have a bachelor's degree and attend the Basic Officer Leadership Course. It can be a long process, but it offers the opportunity to plan and oversee the construction of vast pieces of infrastructure that could serve the nation for years to come.

Training requires fourteen weeks of AIT, which includes practice testing different samples. Soldiers learn to identify health hazards and inspection procedures for food, foodservice operations, wastewater, and waste disposal facilities. Certified apprenticeship programs are available for some specialties in this field. These specialists can go on to careers in local, state, or federal government agencies as food inspectors, public health inspectors, or health and safety inspectors.

MACHINIST

When parts break or wear out on army equipment, it is up to machinists to repair them or create replacements. Machinists create, repair, and modify metal and nonmetal parts using lathes, drill presses, grinders, and other machine shop equipment to do the work. Soldiers in this field should have an interest in math, general science, metalwork, and mechanical drawing. They should be able to apply mathematical formulas and have an interest in making things and solving mechanical problems.

Job training includes twelve weeks of AIT and practice in operating machines. Soldiers learn about machine types and uses, how to set up and operate machines, uses for different metals, and safety procedures. This can lead to civilian machinist careers in factories and repair shops.

The army's construction needs cross many fields. Heavy equipment operators are an important part of the army's many large-scale construction projects. They use machines such as bulldozers, cranes, and loaders to move earth and materials for large projects. Concrete and asphalt equipment operators use some of the same equipment and all equipment related to making asphalt and concrete, using these materials in building projects.

Carpentry and masonry specialists perform general heavy carpentry duties. Plumbers and pipefitters are responsible for installing and repairing pipe systems that carry water, steam, gas, and waste. Metalworkers work with sheet metal and install sheet metal products, such as roofs and air ducts. They also make parts for repairing army watercraft and amphibious vehicles.

CONSTRUCTION

Officers in the construction field plan, design, and direct the building of facilities. Their jobs include studying the need for such facilities, directing surveys of construction areas, designing projects, choosing contractors, and checking the progress of construction. They also plan and direct efforts to modernize and upgrade facilities, plan temporary facilities for emergency use, and keep the master plans for military bases up to date.

Enlisted personnel in machine technology inspect, maintain, and repair military machinery in many categories. They need physical strength and the ability to use hand tools and sophisticated electronic equipment to carry out their jobs.

Track vehicle repairers look after the army's tanks and other vehicles that move on treaded tracks. Their work includes repairing diesel power packs, ignition, fuel, and air induction systems, cooling systems,

A plumber with the 15th Engineer Battalion uses a jig-saw to cut lumber for use in a building project as part of his training.

electrical assemblies, and transmission assemblies. They repair hydraulic brake systems, steering systems, hydraulic assemblies, and fire suppression systems. When track vehicles return from combat, they assess and repair any battlefield damage.

Track vehicle repairers should have an interest in automotive repair, industrial arts, and fixing mechanical problems. They undergo twelve weeks of AIT, during which they learn how to repair, tune up, and replace engines; troubleshoot mechanical and electrical problems; and repair the bodies of track vehicles. This prepares them for careers servicing construction and farm equipment, as well as automobile garage work.

TRANSPORTATION

Wheeled vehicle mechanics maintain and repair the army's wheeled vehicles and associated equipment, such as heavy-wheeled vehicles. These vehicles include Jeeps, trucks, armored combat vehicles, troop transports, and trailers. They test, service, maintain, and repair these vehicles and their components, such as ignition systems, chassis and suspension, transmission, clutch assemblies, brake systems, hydraulic systems, propeller assemblies, and automotive electrical systems. They also perform vehicle recovery operations to bring disabled wheeled vehicles back to base.

Work in this field requires twelve weeks of AIT, during which soldiers learn how to repair and tune up engines; troubleshoot mechanical and electrical problems; repair and replace body panels, fenders, and radiators; and recover malfunctioning or damaged vehicles. This prepares the soldiers for work as mechanics.

Avionic mechanics perform maintenance on tactical communications security, communication, navigation, identification, and flight control equipment on army helicopters and other aircraft. They work on flight controls, stabilization systems, avionics, and controlled cryptographic equipment. Using technical manuals and schematic drawings, they trace wiring harnesses to diagnose, isolate, and repair electrical faults. Their diagnostic and repair work also covers hand tools and measurement and diagnostic equipment.

Training consists of twenty-five weeks of AIT, where soldiers learn how to restore avionic systems and subsystems, as well as repair wiring on aircraft communications, navigation, stabilization, and night-vision imaging systems. They learn basic electronics theory and common soldering and systems installation practices. They will be prepared for work with commercial airlines, aircraft maintenance firms, aircraft manufacturers, and organizations with fleets of airplanes or helicopters.

Soldiers in Iraq work to repair an AH-64 Apache Longbow attack helicopter. Keeping equipment in top working order in a combat zone can be a demanding job.

OTHER MECHANICS JOBS

The army has a vast amount of equipment that must be kept in working order at all times. Careers for mechanics include specialized helicopter repairers for the CH-47 helicopter and the AH-64 attack helicopter, small arms and artillery repairers, construction equipment repairers, and mechanics and specialists for the Bradley fighting vehicle and Avenger weapons systems.

CAREERS FOR OFFICERS

Officers in this field direct personnel in their repair work. They direct repair shop and garage operations, including setting work schedules, overseeing the parts inventory, checking repairs, and supervising the preparation of maintenance records and reports. They develop maintenance standards and policies, plan and develop staff training programs, and brief superior officers on the status of repairs.

CHAPTER 6

LEGAL AND PROTECTIVE SERVICES

All branches of the military have their own legal and protective services systems for the protection of personnel and their families. Military police enforce the laws, army firefighters provide emergency response services, and Judge Advocate General's Corps members provide legal representation and try cases.

MILITARY POLICE

The military police handle crimes committed on army property or that involve army personnel or their families. They enforce military laws and regulations on army installations, control traffic, and respond to emergencies. On the battlefield, they provide support by securing areas, interring prisoners, and conducting police intelligence operations.

Many of their duties are similar to those of civilian police. Military police patrol by car, boat, bicycle, or on foot. They investigate crimes by interviewing witnesses and suspects, collecting evidence, securing crime scenes, and testifying in court. They arrest and charge suspects in crimes, enforce traffic regulations, respond to emergencies, and guard the entrances to military facilities.

Military police undergo nineteen weeks of OSUT, which includes practice in police methods. They learn military and civil laws, jurisdiction, and procedures for investigating crimes and accidents and for controlling traffic and crowds. They also learn how to arrest, restrain, and question suspects and collect evidence. The training and experience can lead to a career with federal, state, or local law enforcement agencies. Military police could also find jobs as security guards at industrial firms, airports, hospitals, or other institutions.

FIREFIGHTER

All army bases have their own fire departments. Army firefighters are responsible for controlling and preventing fires in buildings, aircraft, and ships. Their work is very similar to that of civilian firefighters. They perform rescues and battle flames and smoke during structural fires, vehicle emergencies, aircraft crashes, and natural cover fires like brushfires. They respond to hazardous materials incidents, force their way into burning buildings and vehicles to rescue

Army firefighters are trained to face a wide variety of situations. Here, firefighter trainees put out a fuselage fire on a mock C-130 cargo plane.

personnel, and perform first aid. They inspect aircraft, buildings, and equipment for fire hazards; teach fire protection procedures; and repair firefighting equipment.

Army firefighters are trained at the Department of Defense Fire Academy in San Angelo, Texas, where they undergo thirteen weeks of AIT. Skills they learn include identifying types of fires, fighting fires, conducting rescues, performing first aid, and operating firefighting equipment. These skills prepare army firefighters for future careers with civilian fire departments, as well as with government agencies and civilian firms devoted to protecting life and property during emergencies.

PARALEGAL SPECIALIST

Paralegal specialists help judges, army lawyers, and unit commanders with legal matters and judicial work. They offer support in criminal law, family law, international law, contract law, and fiscal law. They prepare legal documents in military justice matters such as courts-martial and nonjudicial punishment. They tend to administrative law matters, prepare claims processing and investigation, and provide para-legal help in family law, including wills, separation decrees, and powers of attorney.

Paralegals need to be able to type twenty-five words per minute, and those who serve as court reporters must have good hearing and clear speech. Training requirements include ten weeks of AIT, in which soldiers learn legal terminology and research techniques; become acquainted with the army judicial process; and learn how to prepare legal documents, interview witnesses, and summarize transcriptions of legal actions. As civilians, army paralegal specialists

PSYCHOLOGICAL OPERATIONS

Psychological operations are efforts to spread propaganda to influence the emotions, motives, reasoning, and behavior of foreign governments, groups, and individuals. The army uses these efforts to win favor with foreign populations in a way that helps U.S. national security, foreign policy, and diplomatic goals. Psychological operations specialists are active in other countries during conflicts and peacetime.

Psychological operations specialists are able to figure out what kind of information a target population needs in order to create a desired result. They are information and media specialists who are responsible for analyzing, developing, and distributing information used for psychological effect.

This work calls for extensive training, including fourteen weeks of AIT, three weeks of airborne training, and four to six months of language training. These soldiers should have an interest in foreign cultures and languages, and they should have the ability to analyze information, think clearly, and be comfortable in unfamiliar surroundings.

may perform similar work for private law firms, banks, government agencies, insurance companies, and courts.

MILITARY POLICE LIEUTENANT

Military police lieutenants are the officers who direct military police units. They direct support operations, such as surveillance and route reconnaissance for fighting forces. They are in charge of area security, law and order operations, interning and resettlement operations involving U.S. military prisoners and enemy fighters, and police intelligence operations.

They must complete the army's Basic Officer Leader Course II, focusing on leadership duties and responsibilities. They then can move on to the Military Police Basic Officer Leadership Course III, where they learn the functions and responsibilities of the Military Police Corps. This eleven-week course is held at the army's Military Police School at Fort Leonard Wood.

JAG CORPS ATTORNEY

The Judge Advocate General's (JAG) Corps provides legal support to the army. Attorneys in the corps are officers responsible for covering legal matters affecting military operations, including criminal law, labor and employment law, international law, and fiscal law.

Attorneys serve as prosecutors or defense counsel, advise commanders on legal issues, and help soldiers with personal legal matters.

Candidates for the JAG Corps must be U.S. citizens and hold a law degree from an accredited law school. They need to have been admitted to the bar of either a federal court or the highest court in any state or the District of Columbia. They must also be able to serve twenty years of active commissioned service before reaching the age of sixty-two. They undergo a ten-day orientation course, followed by ten-and-a-half weeks of legal training at the Judge Advocate General's Legal Center and School in Charlottesville, Virginia, and six weeks of training through the Direct Commissioned Officers training course, which includes fitness, leadership, and combat training.

CRYPTIC LINGUIST

Cryptic linguists intercept and translate foreign communications. They identify communications from an assigned geographic area and categorize signals by activity type. They analyze these communications for information that can be useful to the army, and they provide transcriptions.

These soldiers undergo three to eighty weeks of special training. Those who are not fluent in a foreign language receive six to eighteen months of foreign

An army attorney speaks with an Iraqi judge through her interpreter and an army linguist as part of an assessment of the local legal system.

language training at the Defense Language Institute before attending AIT. They learn to transcribe communications, identify communications from an assigned geographic area, and categorize signals. They also learn how to analyze foreign communications procedures for preparing reports and handling classified information, and how to use and care for communications equipment.

A soldier shows another how to operate a mobile computer as part of the Global Rapid Response Information Package, which provides remote access to classified and unclassified computer networks.

INTELLIGENCE ANALYST

Intelligence analysts are responsible for making sure that army personnel have access to accurate information about enemy forces and potential combat zones. They take information from a variety of intelligence sources and use it to spot changes in enemy capabilities, vulnerabilities, and possible battlefield scenarios.

They receive and process intelligence reports and messages, help determine the reliability and significance of information, and prepare intelligence reports for commanders. They also create and maintain intelligence records and files and update existing information as new details emerge.

Training for intelligence analysts requires thirteen weeks of AIT and on-the-job instruction, including practice in gathering intelligence. They train in the preparation of maps, charts, and intelligence reports; critical thinking; military symbology, and computer systems. This work can lead to civilian careers with government intelligence agencies, such as the Central Intelligence Agency (CIA) or the National Security Agency (NSA). It can also be helpful in research and business careers.

HUMAN INTELLIGENCE COLLECTOR

Human intelligence collectors gather information about enemies and terrain through interviews and interrogations. They screen sources and documents, debrief and interrogate sources, analyze information and prepare intelligence reports, and help assess threats.

Training includes nineteen weeks of AIT, including practice in gathering intelligence. Soldiers learn to conduct screenings, debriefings, and inter-rogations, and how to manage sources. They also learn to prepare maps and charts, analyze human intelligence, prepare intelligence reports, and use computer systems.

IMAGERY ANALYSTS

Imagery analysts use overhead and aerial imagery, geospatial data, video, and other methods of elec-tronic monitoring to provide the information needed to plan defenses and support combat operations and disaster relief efforts. Their duties include analyzing images created from electronic monitoring sources to identify military installations, facilities, weapon systems, military equipment, and defenses. They deter-mine the precise location and dimensions of objects, identify communication lines and industrial facilities, assess battlefield damage, and prepare imagery analy-sis reports.

Training includes twenty-one weeks of AIT and on-the-job instruction. Analysts learn how to plan imagery collection; prepare maps, charts, and intel-ligence reports; use computer systems and imagery exploitation software; analyze fixed and moving target indicators and geospatial data; and analyze images. The training can prepare soldiers for work within several government agencies, or for careers with engi-neering, mapmaking, mining, or construction firms.

Soldiers working as counterintelligence agents learn valuable skills that can be used in careers with government law enforcement agencies, such as the FBI.

COUNTERINTELLIGENCE AGENTS

Counterintelligence agents supervise and conduct counterintelligence surveys and investigations. Their goal is to detect, assess, and neutralize threats to national security. They investigate and gather information on national security crimes, such as espionage and treason. They prepare the intelligence they gather and distribute it to the necessary parties. They are responsible for meeting with agents and sources, and maintaining counterintelligence files and databases.

Counterintelligence agents are typically recruited from other MOS fields. They undergo nineteen weeks of training at the Counterintelligence Special Agent Course (CISAC). Training includes practice in counterintelligence investigations, operations, and analysis. They learn techniques for conducting interviews and collecting evidence, as well as how to prepare counterintelligence reports, maps, and charts. They also learn to use various computer systems and multidiscipline counterintelligence techniques.

This work prepares soldiers for careers in government agencies, such as the Federal Bureau of Investigation (FBI), CIA, or NSA. Counterintelligence work can also be applied to careers as criminal investigators, detectives, and private investigators. These soldiers may also be interested in careers outside of law enforcement and security, such as in the fields of law, statistics, computer science or programming, reporting, marketing, social work, and counseling.

INTELLIGENCE JOBS FOR OFFICERS

Intelligence officers manage and organize other intelligence specialists and analyze the data they provide. Their duties can include organizing and directing sea, ground, and aerial surveillance; preparing plans to intercept foreign communications; directing analysis of aerial photos and other data; overseeing the writing of intelligence reports; giving briefings on findings; helping plan missions; gathering and analyzing intelligence; and overseeing security investigations.

CHAPTER 7

COMBAT OPERATIONS, LAW ENFORCEMENT, AND SECURITY CAREERS

The U.S. Army's primary objective is to protect the interests of the United States and the lives of its citizens. Soldiers specializing in combat operations are on the front line of the nation's defense. Army law enforcement soldiers support other soldiers and their families by protecting them from crime and providing security at bases and military installations. Intelligence soldiers serve the army's objectives by gathering vital information and making sure that it is interpreted and used properly.

Combat operations are what most people envision when they think of the army. Soldiers go out onto the battlefield, along with those who provide immediate support to them. However, positions in combat operations are only a small percentage of army jobs. Enlisted personnel in this field fight enemies with artillery, assault vehicles, and infantry maneuvers. They carry out scouting missions; operate, clean, and store

An army infantry scout works a security detail during a visit to a high school construction project in Afghanistan's Kapisa Province.

weapons; gather and report information on enemy strengths and locations; drive armored assault vehicles; conduct raids or invasions into enemy territory; and clear mines.

INFANTRYMAN

The infantry is the army's main land combat force. About forty-nine thousand soldiers are members of the infantry. They must be prepared to defend the

GREEN BERETS

Soldiers in the U.S. Army Special Forces are called Green Berets for their distinctive headgear. These soldiers are legendary for their application of unconventional warfare tactics and strategies. The Green Berets are often considered to be the army's elite soldiers. They have six primary missions: unconventional warfare, foreign international defense, special reconnaissance, direct action, hostage rescue, and counterterrorism. They work with foreign troops, take part in combat search-and-rescue missions and manhunts, and serve as peacekeeping forces.

To join the Green Berets, soldiers must meet high fitness standards, score well on the general technical and combat operation sections of the ASVAB, and qualify and volunteer for Airborne training. Once chosen, they endure a grueling twenty-four-day Special Forces Assessment and Selection (SFAS) course consisting of fitness and IQ tests and psychological exams. Only about 40 percent of candidates make it, after which they go through eighteen or twenty-four weeks of intensive language training, followed by twenty-nine to sixty-one weeks of combat tactics and specialty training. Once the training is complete, soldiers are welcomed into one of the world's most elite fighting forces.

United States during peacetime and to repel, capture, and destroy enemy forces during battle. Discipline, high morale, physical stamina, combat skills, and the ability to work as part of a team are highly prized and honed during AIT at Fort Benning.

Infantry soldiers work as members of a team during drills and live combat. While they may have specialties, all infantry soldiers are expected to be able to fire weapons during a fight; perform hand-to-hand combat; help mobilize vehicles, troops, and weapons; and learn to use, maintain, and store combat weaponry such as rifles, machine guns, and antitank mines. They also must be able to operate two-way radios and signal equipment, assist in reconnaissance missions, and process prisoners of war and captured documents.

Requirements for becoming an infantryman include having good vision and hearing. Being physically fit is essential, as infantry soldiers must perform strenuous tasks such as marching with equipment, climbing over obstacles, and digging foxholes. Fourteen weeks of OSUT are required, with most of the training taking place in the field. Infantry soldiers continue to train throughout their army careers by taking part in squad maneuvers, target practice, and war games. The discipline, teamwork, and leadership skills acquired as a member of the infantry can help soldiers succeed in any civilian field they choose.

Currently, the U.S. Army does not allow women to serve as infantry soldiers.

FIRE SUPPORT SPECIALIST

Fire support specialists are members of the army's field artillery team, which supports infantry and tank units in combat by attacking the enemy with weapons that fire large ammunition, rockets, or missiles. Fire support specialists are responsible for finding targets and helping plan artillery strikes. Their duties include preparing and distributing fire support plans and target information, establishing and operating communications systems, encoding and decoding messages, and locating targets using computers or manual calculations. They also operate targeting devices such as laser range finders, and they set up and operate computer systems used to plan and execute attacks. Their work requires that they have normal color vision.

Training requires six weeks of AIT, including time spent in the field under simulated combat conditions. Soldiers learn methods of computing target locations; ammunition techniques; operation of gun, missile, and rocket systems; and artillery tactics, techniques, and procedures. The computer and information technology skills learned and used by these soldiers translate to civilian careers in computer consulting, information technology support, and data processing.

CAVALRY SCOUT

Cavalry scouts are responsible for gathering information on the battlefield. They track and report on enemy troop movements, help direct attacks, and engage the enemy in the field with antiarmor weapons. They perform navigation tasks during combat; work at observation and listening posts; gather and report information on terrain, weather, and the enemy's position and equipment; collect information on routes, tunnels, and bridges; and use principles of camouflage and concealment to stay out of sight.

Working at the Kamdesh Provincial Reconstruction Team Base in Kunar Province in Afghanistan, a cavalry scout carefully scans ridgelines for possible enemy activity.

Cavalry scouts undergo sixteen weeks of OSUT, including nine weeks of basic combat training and seven weeks of specialty training, most of which takes place outside the classroom. Scouts continue training throughout their careers by taking part in squad maneuvers, target practice, and war games.

ARMOR CREWMAN

Tanks and other armored vehicles can turn back enemies on a battlefield through their mobility, firepower, and shock effect. Armor crewmen are members of teams that operate armored equipment, such as the M1A2 Abrams tank and amphibious assault vehicles, to engage the enemy and destroy enemy positions. Crewmembers detect and identify targets, load and fire guns, and operate two-way radios and communications equipment to receive and pass along orders. They take their tracked and wheeled vehicles over all types of terrain and use them to secure battle positions.

To do their job effectively, crewmembers must have the stamina to work long hours in very tight quarters. They also need to be able to choose tank routes and read maps, compasses, and battle plans. Good vision and normal color vision are required for these soldiers.

Armored vehicle crewmembers go through fifteen weeks of OSUT, which includes six weeks of specialized training. Part of this time is spent in the field under simulated combat conditions. Crewmembers are instructed in operating tanks, offensive and defensive tactics, map reading, scouting techniques, and field combat strategies.

AIR AND MISSILE DEFENSE CREWMEMBER

These soldiers are members of the army's air defense artillery team. They use the Avenger weapon system, which is a lightweight and highly mobile surface-to-air rocket system that provides short-range protection against air and land attacks. They have to evaluate targets and operate "friend or foe" identification equipment, prepare the systems for firing, and apply infrared techniques to find and engage targets. They establish radio and wire communications, help maintain situation maps, and resupply ammunition. They need to have normal color vision to identify color-coded ammunition and read maps and charts.

Crewmembers are required to go through ten weeks of AIT and on-the-job instruction. They learn how to compute target locations; handle ammunition; and operate gun, missile, and rocket systems. They are also trained in artillery tactics.

OTHER COMBAT OPERATIONS CAREERS

Combat operations covers many specialized army jobs. These include cannon crewmembers, who work on teams that fire howitzers, which are heavy artillery pieces. Indirect-fire infantrymen fire long-range

Soldiers use a guided missile battery control central vehicle mounted air defense system to fire a Stinger missile at a drone during a live-fire training exercise at Fort Bliss, Texas.

mortars and sometimes have to parachute into position. Field artillery automated tactical data specialists operate data systems for cannons and rocket systems. Patriot missile system teams destroy targets in the air.

Combat operations officers plan and coordinate battles while directing infantry and artillery. They lead troops in raids, demolitions, intelligence gathering, and search-and-rescue operations. These officers should be able to manage and inspire troops and use sound judgment under pressure. Their responsibilities can include gathering and evaluating intelligence on enemy strength and position, developing battle plans, and planning and directing combat operations. They direct the movement of resources in combat zones, and they coordinate artillery and missile strikes. Some officers lead Special Forces teams in missions and train personnel in parachute, scuba, and other special mission techniques.

CHAPTER 8

LIFE AFTER SERVING IN THE ARMY

Leaving the army can be both exciting and terrifying. Whether a soldier has served two years or twenty, he or she must prepare to reenter civilian society once the service contract runs out. Soldiers have to get used to a life without a heavily regimented structure and without the company of longtime comrades. They face many real-world challenges, such as looking for work and finding a place to live. Although the U.S. Department of Veterans Affairs (VA) provides their health care at a low cost, former soldiers must still provide health insurance for their families. Fortunately, they have a wide safety net of army programs to help them with the transition.

Every army post has an Army Career and Alumni Program (ACAP) Center, and every soldier is required to receive preseparation counseling through the center no less than ninety days before leaving the service. The centers help soldiers identify their career

A soldier approaches a police recruiter at a job fair held by the army at Fort Carson, Colorado. Many law enforcement agencies seek out soldiers to fill their ranks.

interests and goals. Counselors help them build résumés that highlight the aspects of their army experience that are most applicable to the chosen career field. They work with soldiers to find locations where their desired jobs are available, and they help soldiers work out such considerations as salary expectations and cost of living.

MEDAL OF HONOR RECIPIENT SALVATORE GIUNTA

Salvatore Giunta served as a staff sergeant in the army during the war in Afghanistan. In November 2010, he became the first living recipient of the Medal of Honor, the military's highest decoration for valor, since the Vietnam War.

Giunta was honored for his actions during a firefight that took place in October 2007. The squad that he was a part of was ambushed after dark by a group of insurgents who attacked with rocket-propelled grenades and AK-47 assault rifles. The soldiers were pinned down and several were wounded. Giunta and the six men under his command attempted to break the assault with grenades. As the insurgents retreated, Giunta saw that they were dragging one of his men with them and gave chase, killing one of the insurgents and bringing his comrade back. Giunta was nominated for the medal two days later.

Some employers specifically seek out former military personnel in the belief that their training and work ethic will serve the company well. The top five military employers are the United Services Automobile Association (USAA), Union Pacific, CSX, BNSF Railway, and ManTech International Corporation.

These companies often send representatives to military job fairs to recruit soldiers preparing to transition out of the service.

THE ARMY RESERVE

Entering the Army Reserve can be a good step for soldiers who are not prepared to leave the military behind. All soldiers who qualify for an honorable discharge must meet with their unit's retention liaison to discuss joining the Army Reserve after the active-duty component of their contract is fulfilled.

Army reservists perform part-time duties, as opposed to active-duty service members. During wartime or at other points when their services are needed, they rotate through mobilizations to active duty. When not on active duty, they perform services or training one weekend per month and during one two-week period per year. As a member of the reserves, a soldier can keep his or her army benefits and even continue to work for promotions to higher rank and learn new skills.

Soldiers should research reserve units near where they want to live to see if their MOS is available, or they should be open to the prospect of switching jobs. They should also think about the impact that a deployment could have just as they are adjusting to civilian life. For example, federal law requires that a reservist's job be kept open while he or she is deployed, but

Medical team members from the 452nd Combat Support Hospital rush an American soldier with shrapnel wounds from a helicopter to the trauma unit at Sunday Olawande Memorial Hospital in Afghanistan.

it may be difficult or stressful to return to a normal job after spending a year deployed in a combat zone. Reservists are paid only for the time that they are active. So when they are not deployed, they receive money only for their monthly drill time and the annual two weeks of service and drills.

CONTINUING EDUCATION

The government offers many options for soldiers who are interested in continuing their education after completing their service. Soldiers can receive college credit or professional credentials for the training they underwent in the army through the American Council on Education (ACE). The ACE reviews military training and experiences, and it awards equivalent college credit to soldiers. More than 2,300 colleges and universities recognize those credits. Soldiers can also qualify for professional licensing and certification in technical fields through their training.

The Tuition Assistance Program (TAP) offers soldiers up to $250 per college credit hour and up to $4,500 per fiscal year for active-duty soldiers who take part in education programs when off duty. This allows soldiers to earn college credits while serving in the army. Also, soldiers who enter the army with debt from student loans up to $65,000 can have them paid off.

The best-known military tuition assistance program is the Montgomery G.I. Bill, which began in 1944 as a way to help veterans returning from World War II. Another bill, called the Post-9/11 G.I. Bill, is available to veterans serving after September 10, 2001, with at least ninety days of continuous service. The program is meant for soldiers serving after the September 11 terrorist attacks, particularly those taking part in the wars in Iraq and Afghanistan. Many soldiers leaving the army today qualify for both programs and must choose between them. However, veterans lose these benefits if they do not use them within ten years of leaving the army.

Under the Montgomery G.I. Bill, qualifying veterans enrolled full-time can receive up to $1,426 per month for a total of $51,000 in tuition for up to thirty-six months. Other rates apply for part-time students and those enrolled in apprenticeship programs

Many programs and opportunities are available to soldiers who are interested in continuing their education, either while still serving or after they reenter civilian life.

or on-the-job training. Soldiers who served less than three years qualify for up to $1,158 per month.

The Post-9/11 G.I. Bill offers soldiers tuition payments equivalent to that of the most expensive state-operated college or university in the state where the veteran's school of choice is located. The program also offers a monthly housing allowance and a stipend for books. Active-duty soldiers who take advantage of the program while still serving can be compensated for the entire cost of their tuition regardless of the price.

The army also takes care of soldiers who entered the service with outstanding college debt. Programs are available to help soldiers repay loans of up to $65,000.

THE TRANSITION ASSISTANCE PROGRAM

Finding a job and deciding to continue one's education are both major decisions. The army, in addition to helping soldiers find jobs and pay for their education, assists with broader aspects of their return to civilian life. Operated by the Departments of Defense, Labor, and Veterans Affairs, the Transition Assistance Program is designed to help soldiers plan their futures.

The Wounded Warrior Program provides a support network for injured soldiers transitioning out of the army. Here, a veteran is shown with a service dog provided by the program.

The program helps former soldiers find a new place to live by providing information on military communities and offering housing workshops. Former soldiers are encouraged to determine their needs and means and develop a relocation plan. The program also assists in planning financial strategies.

Soldiers cease receiving pay from the army as soon as they take off their uniform. The program can help soldiers and their families manage a limited income while the soldier looks for work. Group seminars and workshops are offered to help soldiers deal with unexpected costs, such as the price of health insurance.

The army also has the Wounded Warrior Program, which aids soldiers who have been severely wounded. The program works on behalf of severely wounded, ill, and injured soldiers, veterans, and their families. It helps these soldiers make the transition to veteran status and works to foster the wounded soldier's independence through a trained advocate assigned to each soldier.

GLOSSARY

artillery Large, powerful guns used by an army; they are moved on wheels or fixed in one place.

avionics Electronics designed for use in aircraft.

barracks A building or set of buildings used to house soldiers.

convoy A group of vehicles traveling together for protection.

cryptographic Relating to the coding and decoding of messages and communications.

dietetics The science of applying the principles of nutrition to food preparation.

drill The act of training soldiers to march and handle a weapon in a particular way.

extrication The act of freeing or removing someone or something from an entanglement or difficulty.

geospatial Of or relating to the relative position of things on Earth's surface.

hypertension Abnormally high blood pressure.

infrastructure The system of public works of a city, state, or country.

linguist A person who speaks and studies many languages.

morale The confidence, enthusiasm, and discipline of a person or group at a particular time.

munitions Military weapons, ammunition, equipment, and stores.

platoon A small military unit usually consisting of three sections of ten to twelve men.

pneumatic Operating by air or by the pressure or exhaustion of air.

propaganda Information, ideas, or rumors deliberately spread to help or harm a person, group, movement, nation, or other institution.

radiological Involving radioactive materials.

reconnaissance A search for useful military information in the field, particularly on the ground.

tactic A plan for producing a desired result.

FOR MORE INFORMATION

Army Historical Foundation

2425 Wilson Boulevard

Arlington, VA 22201

(800) 506-2672

Web site: http://www.armyhistory.org

The Army Historical Foundation is dedicated to preserving the history and heritage of the American soldier.

Canadian War Museum

1 Vimy Place

Ottawa, ON K1A 0M8

Canada

(819) 776-8600

Web site: http://www.warmuseum.ca

The Canadian War Museum depicts Canada's military past and how it shaped the country.

Department of National Defence and Canadian Forces

Major-General George R. Pearkes Building

101 Colonel By Drive

Ottawa, ON K1A 0K2

Canada

(613) 995-2534

Web site: http://forces.gc.ca
The Department of National Defence and Canadian Forces is responsible for all matters concerning Canadian defense.

Stars and Stripes

529 14th Street NW, Suite 350

Washington, DC 20045-1301

(202) 761-0900

Web site: http://www.stripes.com
Stars and Stripes is a news service dedicated to providing news and information to the U.S. military community.

U.S. Department of Defense

1400 Defense Pentagon

Washington, DC 20301-1400

(703) 571-3343

Web site: http://www.defense.gov
The U.S. Department of Defense encompasses the army and the other four branches that make up the nation's military.

U.S. Department of Veterans Affairs

810 Vermont Avenue NW

Washington, DC 20420

(202) 461-7600

Web site: http://www.va.gov
The mission of the U.S. Department of Veterans Affairs is to see that soldiers get the benefits and services that they have earned.

U.S. Military Academy at West Point

Garrison Commander, Building 681

U.S. Military Academy

West Point, NY 10996

(845) 938-3808

Web site: http://www.usma.edu

West Point is the army's premier training ground for future officers.

WEB SITES

Due to the changing nature of Internet links, Rosen Publishing has developed an online list of Web sites related to the subject of this book. This site is updated regularly. Please use this link to access the list:

http://www.rosenlinks.com/cod/army

FOR FURTHER READING

Adams, Simon. *Soldier*. New York, NY: DK Publishing, 2009.

Carlisle, Rodney P. *Afghanistan War*. Philadelphia, PA: Chelsea House Publications, 2010.

Center for Army Leadership. *The U.S. Army Leadership Field Manual*. New York, NY: McGraw-Hill, 2004.

Dalessandro, Robert J. *Army Officer's Guide*. Harrisburg, PA: Stackpole Books, 2009.

David, Jack. *United States Army*. Minneapolis, MN: Bellwether Media, 2008.

Department of the Army. *The Soldier's Guide*. New York, NY: Skyhorse Publishing, 2007.

Department of the Army. *U.S. Army Counterintelligence Handbook*. Guilford, CT: Lyons Press, 2004.

Dolan, Edward F. *Careers in the U.S. Army*. Tarrytown, NY: Marshall Cavendish Benchmark, 2008.

Gay, Kathlyn. *The Military and Teens: The Ultimate Teen Guide*. Lanham, MD: Scarecrow Press, 2008.

Goldish, Meish. *Army: Civilian to Soldier*. New York, NY: Bearport Publishing, 2010.

Herbert, Don. *63 Days and a Wake-Up: Your Survival Guide to United States Army Basic Combat Training*. Bloomington, IN: iUniverse, 2007.

Larsen, Matt. *U.S. Army Survival Handbook*. Guilford, CT: Lyons Press, 2008.

Ostrow, Scott A. *Mastering the ASVAB*. Lawrenceville, NJ: Peterson's Publishing, 2008.

Peckyno, Ryan. *West Point Military Academy*. Pittsburgh, PA: College Prowler, 2005.

Rice, Earle, Jr. *The U.S. Army and Military Careers*. Berkeley Heights, NJ: Enslow Publishers, 2007.

Rustad, Martha E. *U.S. Army Infantry Fighting Vehicles*. Mankato, MN: Capstone Press, 2006.

Schumacher, Gerry. *To Be a U.S. Army Green Beret*. Minneapolis, MN: Zenith Publishing, 2005.

Storlie, Chad. *Combat Leader to Corporate Leader: 20 Lessons to Advance Your Civilian Career*. Toronto, ON, Canada: Praeger, 2010.

Vanderhoof, Gabrielle. *Army Rangers*. Philadelphia, PA: Mason Crest Publishers, 2010.

Volkin, Michael. *The Ultimate Basic Training Handbook: Tips, Tricks, and Tactics for Surviving Boot Camp*. El Dorado Hills, CA: Savas Beatie, 2007.

BIBLIOGRAPHY

CNN. "Obama Signs Repeal of 'Don't Ask, Don't Tell' Policy." December 22, 2010. Retrieved March 1, 2011 (http://articles.cnn.com/2010-12 22/politics/dadt.repeal_1_repeal-openly-gay-men-president-barack-obama?_s=PM:POLITICS).

Department of the Army. *The Soldier's Guide*. New York, NY: Skyhorse Publishing, 2007.

Farley, Janet I. *Military-to-Civilian Career Transition Guide*. Indianapolis, IN: JIST Publishing, 2010.

GoArmy.com. "Careers and Jobs: Combat." Retrieved March 1, 2011 (http://www.goarmy.com/careers-and-jobs/browse-career-and-job-categories/combat.html).

GoArmy.com. "Careers and Jobs: Intelligence and Combat Support." Retrieved March 1, 2011 (http://www.goarmy.com/careers-and-jobs/browse-career-and-job-categories/intelligence-and-combat-support.html).

GoArmy.com. "Careers and Jobs: Legal and Law Enforcement." Retrieved March 1, 2011 (http://www.goarmy.com/careers-and-jobs/browse-career-and-job-categories/legal-and-law-enforcement.html).

GoArmy.com. "Introduction to the U.S. Army Medical Department." Retrieved March 1, 2011 (http://www.armymedicine.army.mil/about/introduction.html).

Harris, Bill. *The Complete Idiot's Guide to Careers in the U.S. Military*. Indianapolis, IN: Pearson Education, 2002.

Henderson, C. J., and Jack Dolphin. *Career Opportunities in the Armed Forces*. New York, NY: Checkmark Books, 2007.

Junger, Sebastian. *War*. New York, NY: Twelve, 2010.

Kenyon, Henry. "Army Cyber Unit Stands Guard Over Computer Networks." DefenseSystems.com, October 14, 2010. Retrieved March 1, 2011 (http://www.defensesystems.com/Articles/2010/10/15/Cyber-Defense-Army-Cyber-Command.aspx).

Lee, Jesse. "President Obama Presents the Medal of Honor to Staff Sergeant Salvatore Giunta." White House Blog, November 16, 2010. Retrieved March 1, 2011 (http://www.whitehouse.gov/blog/2010/11/16/president-obama-presents-medal-honorstaff-sergeant-salvatore-giunta-we-re-all-your-).

Ostrow, Scott A. *Guide to Joining the Military*. Lawrenceville, NJ: Thomson Learning, 2004.

Ronson, Jon. *The Men Who Stare at Goats*. New York, NY: Simon & Schuster, 2006.

Rostker, Bernard. *I Want You! The Evolution of the All-Volunteer Force*. Santa Monica, CA: RAND Corporation, 2006.

Rubin, Elizabeth. "In One Moment in Afghanistan, Heroism and Heartbreak." New York Times, November 13, 2010. Retrieved March 1, 2011 (http://www.nytimes.com/2010/11/14/weekinreview/14rubin.html?_r=1).

Sackett, Paul R., and Ann S. Mavor, eds. *Assessing Fitness for Military Enlistment*. Washington, DC: National Academies Press, 2006.

Schading, Barbara. *A Civilian's Guide to the U.S. Military*. Cincinnati, OH: Writer's Digest Books, 2007.

U.S. Army. "The Official Homepage of the United States Army." Retrieved March 1, 2011 (http://www.army.mil).

Vaughn, Kirby Lee. *The Enlistment Planning Guide*. Santa Barbara, CA: Essayons Publishing, 1995.

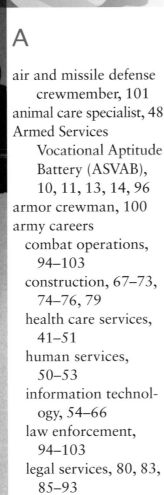

INDEX

pharmacy specialist, 48
Post-9/11 G.I. Bill, 110, 112
post-traumatic stress disorder (PTSD), 8
preventive medicine specialist, 49
psychological operations specialist, 84

R

radiology specialist, 49
radio operations jobs, 61–63
Reserve Officers' Training Corps (ROTC), 18
respiratory specialist, 48

S

satellite communications systems operator-maintainer, 58–60
Signal Corps, 39, 40, 60–61
signal support systems specialist, 57–58
small arms and artillery repairer, 78
social worker, 51, 53
special electronic devices repairer, 63–65
Special Forces, 96, 103
specialized helicopter repairer, 78

T

track vehicle repairer, 74, 76

Transition Assistance Program, 112–114
transportation jobs, 76–77
Tuition Assistance Program (TAP), 110

U

U.S. Army
    basic and skill training, 23–40
    enlisting, 7–22
    life after, 6, 7, 104–114
    overview, 4–6
U.S. Army Corps of Engineers, 72
U.S. Army Reserve, 107–109
U.S. Department of Defense, 10, 33, 34, 40, 82, 112
U.S. Department of Labor, 112
U.S. Department of Veterans Affairs, 104, 112
U.S. Military Academy, 18

V

veterinary food inspection specialist, 48

W

water treatment specialist, 67, 71–73
wheeled vehicle mechanic, 76
women, in the army, 5, 10, 98
World War II, 110
Wounded Warrior Program, 114

ABOUT THE AUTHOR

Jason Porterfield is a journalist and writer living in Chicago, Illinois. He graduated from Oberlin College, where he majored in English, history, and religion. He has written more than twenty books for Rosen Publishing on various topics, including several covering historical subjects and the U.S. military. His titles include *Careers as a Cyberterrorism Expert*, *USAF Special Tactics Teams*, and *The Treaty of Guadalupe-Hidalgo, 1848*.

PHOTO CREDITS

Cover (top, bottom middle), pp. 1 (top, bottom middle), 3, 15, 21, 24, 29, 31, 35, 36, 42, 68, 75, 78, 82, 88 Photo Courtesy of U.S. Army; cover (bottom left, bottom right), pp. 1 (bottom left, bottom right), 44, 46, 56, 57, 59, 64, 70, 87, 95, 99, 102 http://www.defenseimagery.mil; p. 5 © Craig F. Walker/The Denver Post/ZUMApress.com; pp. 7, 23, 41, 54, 67, 80, 94, 104 xiver/Shutterstock.com; pp. 9, 13, 17, 111 © AP Images; pp. 18, 37, 49, 63, 72, 84, 96, 106, 115, 117, 120, 122, 125 U.S. Navy photo; p. 27 Chris Hondros/Getty Images; p. 38 Maxim Marmur/AFP/Getty Images; pp. 52, 105 John Moore/Getty Images; p. 91 FBI; p. 108–109 Scott Olson/Getty Images; p. 113 © Corey Perrine/The Augusta Chronicle/ZUMApress.com; back cover http://www.dvidshub.net/; multiple interior graphics Losswen/Shutterstock.com.

Designer: Les Kanturek; Editor: Nicholas Croce; Photo Researcher: Amy Feinberg